PRAISE FOR A

"*The Anthropologists* is yet a
book from Ayşegül Savaş: she is an author who simply, and astoundingly, knows. Savaş knows hope. Savaş knows despair. Savaş knows joy, and malaise, and laughter, and curiosity. There are worlds inside of Savaş's prose, and *The Anthropologists* is both a bright light and a map for how to be. A massively heartening achievement."

—Bryan Washington, author of *Memorial*

"Like Walter Benjamin, Ayşegül Savaş uncovers trapdoors to bewilderment everywhere in everyday life; like Henry James, she sees marriage as a mystery, unsoundably deep. *The Anthropologists* is mesmerizing; I felt I read it in a single breath."

—Garth Greenwell, author of *Cleanness*

"[Savaş] writes with both sensuality and coolness, as if determined to find a rational explanation for the irrationality of existence."

—Sarah Lyall, *The New York Times*

"*White on White* is marvelous, as elegant as an opaque sheet of ice that belies the swift and turbulent waters beneath."

—Lauren Groff, author of *Matrix*

"Savaş's restrained style is a statement in itself, minimalist on the surface but more textured than what first meets the eye."

—Michele Filgate, *Los Angeles Times*

"A haunting, irresistible novel. I loved this book for its depth and perception, for its beauty and eerie rhythms, but most of all for its wonderfully dreamlike spell. It's breathtaking."

—Brandon Taylor, author of *The Late Americans*

"In the Middle Ages, human skin was seen as a blanket stretched to cover a secret, inner life, writes Ayşegül Savaş. Reading *White on White* for me is like an outer skin which you open layer by layer as you read; gentle, mysterious and profound."

—Marina Abramović

THE WILDERNESS

AYŞEGÜL SAVAŞ

TRANSIT
BOOKS

Published by Transit Books
1250 Addison St #103, Berkeley, CA 94702
www.transitbooks.org

Cover design by Anna Morrison | Typesetting by Transit Books
Printed in the United States of America

9 8 7 6 5 4 3 2 1

This project is supported in part by a grant from the
National Endowment for the Arts.

for my mother

THE

WILDERNESS

1.

My mother arrived to Paris from Istanbul the day before I gave birth, but wasn't allowed to visit us at the hospital. She couldn't sleep from excitement; she walked from our apartment to the hospital several times a day, pacing up and down the emergency entrance, while I labored for twenty-four hours.

On the day we were discharged, a kind nurse permitted my mother to come up to the room, to help us carry our bags. She burst inside and ran toward the baby. What I remember is that she didn't kiss me. She didn't come to her own child first.

But in truth, I remember very little. In truth, I have already forgotten everything.

2.

Ahead of her arrival, my mother had sent us a package. In it were blankets and washcloths for the baby, nursing pajamas for me, a sweater for my husband, and an ugly red satin headband with a ribbon. The last, she explained laughing on the phone, was for me to wear during labor.

In the final month of my pregnancy, those weeks of aches, the blurry taking leave from life, lying awake at night, I'd begun to inquire about the mythology surrounding the first forty days after birth, an important period in Turkish culture, considered one of extreme fragility for the mother and baby alike.

My friend Katia, a doula living in the French Belledonne Mountains, had sent me a book of recipes for the postpartum period, which my husband read out to me in bed. The book, inspired by traditional Chinese medicine, also advocated for forty days of rest for the new mother, alongside recipes for fortifying broths and stews. In this time, the authors wrote, the cold and wind were to be strictly avoided.

In Turkish mythology, too, the new mother was susceptible to air currents that often brought with them invisible beings. One of these beings was the

Scarlet Woman, a demon who often took the form of a human and attacked the postpartum mother and baby. Going into labor wearing something red was one way to ward her off. It was for this reason that my mother—a pediatrician—had sent me the headband. I asked her on the phone whether she believed in this stuff.

"Of course not," she said. But she added that many women at her hospital labored with a red item of clothing. It sounded as if she wanted to take all precautions, just in case.

On video, I asked my grandmother whether she'd heard of the Scarlet Woman.

"Of course," she said, "but those things only happen in villages."

My grandmother's caretaker, listening to the conversation, chimed in that the Scarlet Woman would appear in the evenings. You would know of her presence by something very heavy and dark pressing down on your chest.

I asked whether she had been visited after the births of her children. The caretaker shook her head, repeating the name of Allah.

3.

We walk back home from the hospital, the same way we walked four days ago for the induction. My belly was so low it was almost touching my thighs. But even at that final hour, I was hopping on one foot, trying to start the labor. The previous afternoon, I had swum a kilometer, run up and down the stairs of our building, then stayed up all night meditating, telling the baby it was all right to come now, that we were ready for her. I wanted desperately for the birth to happen naturally, with an idea that things would otherwise be off to a bad start. At the hospital, I begged to be given some more time, even as they were administering the hormone to start contractions.

Headed back home, I'm holding the baby in her bear suit, two fluffy ears swallowing the little head. I am wearing my pregnancy jeans, the same ones I wore on the way to induction, now a little looser around the belly.

During the ten-minute walk, no one greets us or looks in our direction. We are, after all, not an unusual sight. But I have grown used to gazes from strangers, beams of approval at my belly, random acts of kindness. Halfway home, I have to stop and hand over the baby to my mother, overcome with fatigue.

My face, in the photographs my husband took that day, is swollen and translucent. Zooming in on a photo some days later, I notice that I have a line of soft hair along my jaw. I ask my husband whether I have always had this.

"What?" my husband asks.

"This. This hair."

He shrugs. He tells me it's just a continuation of my hairline.

I ask my mother.

"Oh it's nothing," she says, though she knits her eyebrows to examine carefully. She then adds, in no way relieving me, that if it were a hormonal disorder, I would have thick black hairs.

"This is just fuzz," she says. "Like a quince."

I feel I'm deforming by the minute, that the hair will sprout all the way down my neck and torso, making me animal. I remember in panic that I had once written of such a scene, in which a character's mental breakdown arrives with nightmares of fur sprouting down her neck. I have the feeling that I've somehow brought this upon myself.

Days later, as I sweat through layers of towels

stacked on the mattress, I shed the fur, shed all the
soft hairs on my forearms. One night, I have a night-
mare that my eyebrows fall off, and my eyelashes
too.

4.

Our first evening at home, as my husband and I are
sitting down for the dinner my mother prepared, the
baby begins to cry again. All day, we have tended to
her needs. All day, I have waited for a beginning: for
the baby to reveal itself to me. To know who she is,
or what, exactly, she wants.

"What's she crying about now?" I ask my mother, who is holding the baby by the kitchen counter
while we eat lentil-and-meatball soup.

"Oh, anything and everything," my mother says.

I haven't slept in four days. Even longer, if you
count the sleepless nights leading up to labor. I'm
waiting for our life to begin with order and a dis-
cernible shape. Meanwhile, my mother is waiting to
present me with the suitcase of gifts she's brought
from Istanbul. This is the most pressing task for her,
never mind the crying baby, which she accepts with

some sort of cheer, as if the baby is just being silly. I keep putting off the delivery of gifts; I cannot be bothered, but I do retain a glimmer of surprise at my own lack of interest, I who love gifts. *So this is how it is*, I think, like I've discovered a new disposition, a future of not caring.

The following morning, when the baby is sleeping in my husband's arms, my mother comes into our bedroom with a large bag. From its depths she retrieves items one by one, announcing their provenance: From Aunt Oya. From Aunt Gülhan. From Uncle Bekir. There are gold coins, given at birth and marriage and circumcision. There are handmade sweaters and blankets. There are little animal toys, many of them rabbits.

My mother has also knit the baby cardigans and vests and booties and hats. These are the ones we will favor in the months ahead, the ones that will mark the period of the baby's emergence from animal to human, their bright colors and serene shapes so at odds with the chaos I'm harboring.

Once she has presented almost everything, my mother takes out her last gifts. For me, a turquoise ring she had made at the Armenian jeweler whose grandfather made my great-grandmother's wedding earrings. For the baby: a necklace and earring set given to my mother by her mother-in-law. I have always loved these jewels. She wants the baby to have them, she says, but of course I can wear them in the meantime.

I feel embarrassed by the presents, of being fattened up like this, honored. I feel I will now have to prove myself, step into my new role as bejeweled matron.

One summer years ago, my eccentric and enthusiastic grandfather presented me with a strange totem he'd made, of a woman's head attached to a wolf's body, two strands of garlic hanging on either side. He explained that it represented a mother's love, fierce as a wolf, and that I would become whole in motherhood. At the end of the summer, angered and ashamed, I left the totem wrapped in a plastic bag on top of the minibar in a hotel room. A few years later, after my brother's engagement, my grandfather told my American sister-in-law that, although we loved her very much as a family, we would love her even more if she were to give birth. He asked my brother to translate his words.

"We're so happy to welcome you into our family," my brother said.

I put the gifts aside, tell my mother I want to rest. I'm still waiting for the one stretch of sleep that will finally help me recover. It will not come. For months after, every time I tip past sanity, I will cry that I have not recovered from birth. But my pleas of exhaustion will lose their potency, so often repeated, stretched so far past the birth. My crying will slope toward madness.

5.

In Anatolian mythology, the Scarlet Woman pertains to the species of the jinn, the spirits of the invisible realm that can nonetheless manifest themselves to humans. The Prophet has said that God divided the human and jinn into ten parts. One part makes up the human race, and nine the jinn. In Arabic, the letters *jeem* and *nuun* combined signify what is invisible, or hidden. Paradise, for example, is *Jannah*; *janeen* means fetus.

In the Quran, the jinn are addressed as nations bestowed with rationality, capable of understanding the word of God. For this reason, they will bear witness on the Day of Judgment. As humans are created of clay, so jinn are made of air: "Indeed We have created man out of sounding clay, out of black mud molded into shape, whereas the jinn We had created before him out of the fire of scorching winds."

In the book of recipes Katia sent us, the postpartum mother is warned, above all, to avoid the wind. Her own constitution, recently hollowed by birth, is air. Any more and she will surely lose her grounding, begin to float.

6.

Those first days, our telephones are flooded with messages. I glance at mine without responding to anything. My husband and my mother offer theirs in batches: congratulations from Aunt Sermin, Uncle Fuat, Kerime, Leo, Primoz. They send their love. They ask after me.

"Thanks," I say.

There is one message that causes me particular panic, especially when it comes from other mothers. They congratulate me on the baby. They tell me how beautiful she is. They say that I must be so happy.

7.

The Scarlet Woman may be a manifestation of Lilith, who appears in the Bible as Adam's disobedient first wife. In Isaiah, she lives in the desert land of the Edomites: "Wildcats shall meet hyenas / Goat-demons shall greet each other / There too the lilith shall repose / And find herself a resting place."

Some historians trace Lilith to the Sumerian epic of Gilgamesh, from around 2000 BCE: The goddess Inanna's plans to make her throne from a willow tree are prevented when a serpent and Zu bird build their nests in the tree and the demoness Lilitu takes residence in its trunk. The hero Gilgamesh slays the dragon. The Zu bird flies away and Lilitu flees to the desert.

Lilitu derives from the Sumerian *lil*, meaning *phantom*. In the first millennium BCE, the same word is used to denote the wind as well. In Jewish demonology, Lilith is believed to endanger women in childbirth and kill their offspring, like her Sumerian counterpart Labratu, a creature in the guise of a long-haired woman who sucks the blood of babies.

In the Greek Testament of Solomon from the third century, a female demon is said to roam the world at night, strangling newborns.

A Hebrew inscription found in northern Syria dating from about the eighth century BCE: "To her that flies in rooms of darkness—pass quickly, quickly, Lil[ith]."

In the King James Bible, *Lilith* is translated as *the screech owl*, recalling her home in the tree and her nocturnal wanderings.

8.

Nighttime descends like a fair: with its different rooms and attractions, the varying atmospheres. As light fades, the baby begins to cry more ardently. One person goes to the guest room with the baby while the other two eat. At ten, I sleep for an hour. At eleven, my mother goes to bed for the night. From then on, my husband and I take three-hour shifts holding the baby in the living room, because she will only sleep if she is being held. Whenever we try putting her down, she wakes up immediately, furious. She will not fall back asleep, suspicious that we may abandon her again.

Insomnia, which has haunted my sleep for years, vanishes like a fleeing spirit. I fall asleep within seconds of lying down. In my dreams, my husband comes into the bedroom and stands by the bed. He says it's time. I wake up in panic, the room is empty, and I worry that I am late to take over. I rush to the living room to start my shift.

"Why are you here?" my husband asks. "It's still early."

He tells me to go back to bed and not get up until he comes for me, not believe the dreams. I agree. Immediately, I fall back asleep but am soon roused by the phantom of the baby to whom I must return.

"Jinn avenge their dead by inflicting upon humans strange sounds," writes Amira El-Zein in her study of jinn in Islamic culture. "The sounds produced by the jinn could be similar to the pounding of a drum, the buzzing of certain flies, a twitter, or simply a loud voice coming from an invisible source the Arabs called *hatif* (a call from the unseen)."

I tell my mother about my hallucinations.

"That's what I call responsibility," my mother says. I had hoped she might say it is the indisputable sign of my bond with the baby. Whereas responsibility seems so cold, so unlike the alchemy I have imagined.

9.

On one of our first mornings, once the turbulence of night has passed and the baby is soundly asleep, my mother goes around the apartment putting bowls of nuts and dried fruits on tables and at our bedside. There are roasted chickpeas, hazelnuts, mulberries. Walnuts lined on a string, dipped in grape molasses. It occurs to me that she has imagined this scene, the loveliness of this time together and of nourishing us.

After breakfast, we light candles and sit in the living room, sunshine streaming on the baby, who has hid her face in my armpit. I remember this, because there are photographs from that day, our home beautiful and orderly. A picture of perfect calm though I have no bodily recollection of it.

I send photos to friends: the baby sleeping, wrapped in lovely blankets. Rooms with candles and bowls of fruits. In parallel, I am immersed in a constant correspondence with other mothers, frantically asking for solace, for ways out of this wilderness in which I find myself trapped.

"Was it like this for you?" I ask. "Did you feel a little out of it? Is breastfeeding supposed to be excruciating?"

My friend Catherine, with whom I have been discussing milk supply, responds:

"Is it kind of disorienting how the beautiful quietude of these photos can contrast with the fear and pain and upheaval?"

10.

A delivery arrives from our friend Chiara, herself about to give birth: jars of broth, boxes of porridge, chicken-and-quince stew, dozens of muffins. I sit at the table and cry. My mother, sitting across from me, watches in silence. After a while, she gets up and goes to her room.

In the bedroom, choking in tears, I tell my husband that my mother must not have wanted me at birth.

"Why would you say that?" he asks. "That's obviously not true."

"Do you see how she's immune to my crying? Do you see how she ignores me?"

I tell him repeatedly that I've lost my mother, a refrain which grows stronger each night. But my mother is here, cooking and cleaning for us.

Changing the baby and dressing her, holding her in the mornings when my husband and I sleep for two hours. Still, the loss feels insurmountable, though I begin to suspect that my mother stands for something larger, a loss of many things. I turn everything against my mother, whatever loss this is that is about to swallow me.

That night, before she goes to bed, I begin to cry again. My mother looks away—tactful or embarrassed or exasperated. In any case, not knowing what to do about me.

The word that comes out of my mouth is a surprise for us both. It is a little old-fashioned, a little sentimental. It doesn't pertain to my lexicon.

"Why are you so *merhametsiz*?" I ask. Without mercy.

My mother says she is afraid to say anything. I rebuff whatever she does. I'm always on edge. I cannot be approached.

"What sort of mother doesn't kiss her child after she gives birth?" I sob.

The next morning, I text Katia that I feel bad for lashing out at my mother.

"Don't feel bad," she writes. "This is a time for mothering."

In her 1975 essay "Ghosts in the Nursery," psycho-analyst Selma Fraiberg distinguishes between the types of ghosts that appear after birth. Some are transient, whereas others remain, interfering. It is these stubborn ghosts, who live in the mother's past, that must be located and swept away, so that they may leave her and the baby in peace.

The family mythology of my early years is so familiar to me that it has eroded to a cliché. My brother and I are born a year apart; my father is perpetually, pathologically, away; my mother is doing her pediatrics residency. By the time we are toddlers, my mother is working night shifts at the hospital, arriving home exhausted in the early mornings to her eager, demanding children. We ask her, "Why must you be the mother of other babies?" There is her mother-in-law, who takes care of us but treats our mother as a second-class citizen. It is a hellish time, though the anecdotes have somehow been passed down in humor, as punch lines.

I'm gripped by a fear that my crying indicates something terrible. In the minutes I have to myself, I try to concentrate on the ghosts of my childhood, to find something that clicks.

"The apparition is a state of mind," writes artist

Himali Singh Soin in her manifesto on translucency, "in which the lens of time has a soft focus, a peripheral vision that allows you to see the microscopic and the grand scale of things at once."

Am I crying for myself or for my mother? Am I crying for the baby haunted by my childhood self?

"To be ghost," says Singh Soin, "is to be generous with boundaries. The ghost story allows us to construct a language of translucency: both *is* and *can be*."

I cannot arrive at anything specific; no memory to reveal my state to me, as the ubiquitous logic of popular psychology demands. It is this same logic that has set me on the path to solving the problem. This idea that sadness must be hunted down and eradicated, and that it can be done by looking back and finding the culprit. But I'm too tired. Rather than confronting the feeling head on, I puncture it occasionally, letting it deflate, until it expands and fills me again. Over and over again, I am seized by sadness and anger, a wish to be cared for and an inability to accept care.

I set strict rules about my mother's rest. At eleven every night, I order her to go to bed, and not to get up until seven in the morning, though I myself have barely slept in over a week. My bleeding is so strong I wonder if I might hemorrhage, or drop the baby from my exhausted arms. Every afternoon, I tell my mother to go out, go to the Seine, to Saint-Sulpice, to the Luxembourg Gardens, to the flea market. She accepts, hesitantly, telling us she is worried that we may need her in her absence.

"No!" I say. "We'll be absolutely fine."

When she returns from her outings, she starts to clean and cook in a frenzy. The more tired I am, the more I cry, the more she seems to scrub floors and thicken her soups: lentils, meatballs, yogurt, eggs, pasta. She scoffs at the foods my husband and I prioritize, from the book Katia sent us. Beer yeast, bone broth, fennel tea. My mother has found her own shops, different from the ones where my husband and I go: a Tunisian butcher, the Lebanese grocer brothers.

One afternoon, she sets about making a red, spicy sherbet, cooked over days with many cups of sugar. It's a postpartum drink, meant to increase milk. She brings me a mug, the top covered in crushed walnuts. I sip obligingly, though I find it sickeningly sweet. In traditional homes, this sherbet would be served to guests. But this isn't a traditional home.

We've had no visitors, except for the midwife who came to check my stitches. We have no family in Paris. A few close friends propose coming over to meet the baby. We tell them it's too early, that we can barely get through a single day, and they say, of course, they understand. This is the way of our lives here: full of understanding and boundaries. No relatives showing up unannounced, no one staying past their welcome or sleeping over. There is no excess of food and advice. No unwanted hands cuddling the baby. These are the problems of the early postpartum back home. For us, there are no extra hands to help and to hold, either, no lighthearted cousins with whom to chatter. No other human scents our baby can trust.

11.

Everything, it seems to me, everything in the world, is about breast milk. Whenever aunts and cousins call to ask how we are doing, I want only to hear whether they breastfed their children. I ask it of everyone, listing to my mother every female we know. How have I managed to avoid these facts my whole life, when it's a matter of life and death? How have I never known this particular language of nourishment?

"My milk dried up in a day from grief," one aunt tells me.

"At the end of the summer, my milk went sour from the heat and made the baby sick."

"I had so much, my breasts were sore for weeks."

Every time the baby feeds—eight, nine, ten times a day—I cry from the pain. I have an open wound, dug into every two hours. The baby yanks at the bleeding nipples, never getting enough and never letting go. I grind my teeth through the whole thing, get up with shaky legs to dab cream at my breasts though they are too swollen to touch.

On the sixth day, after days of resisting formula in hopes that my milk will increase, we discover that the baby has lost more weight. I call a lactation consultant. She arrives with an old-fashioned leather bag like a stage prop. She asks me to show her how I feed the baby. I wrap the large, serpentine cushion around me, take the baby in my arms, and position her nose level with the breast, mouth facing up, my arm keeping her body steady. This is the way to achieve a painless latch, I've been told, by my mother and breastfeeding manuals, and the doctors at the hospital. The pain is so great I would rather be giving birth all day long.

The baby latches on, I yelp, then stifle my pain in front of the stranger.

"Ah," the consultant says calmly. "You see how the baby is contorted?" She takes her in her arms, waits for the screaming to subside, then positions her on my side, the head peeping out of my armpit. She supports her back with one hand while the baby calmly sucks.

The pain is there, but bearable.

"Just a simple fix," she responds to my frantic gratitude.

After the work is done, my mother offers her a cup of the red sherbet.

"This is our traditional drink," she says in English, which I translate to French. The midwife says it tastes a lot like Christmas tea. She is suspicious that it will increase my milk supply but, she says, at least it's nice and sugary. When she's leaving, she suggests that I pump milk in my free time.

"I don't have free time," I almost shout. "The baby's always feeding. It already hurts so much."

"Ah," she says. "It's true you need rest as well."

Nothing, in this time, is ever resolved. Questions hover about with contradictions and counterarguments: That I am angry at my mother and want to sit talking to her all day. That she was very tired and angry in my childhood and that she loved us very much. That I need to rest, urgently, and that I'm afraid for the baby, and want to be close to her. Each evening, as the baby and I begin to cry, my mother and husband discuss the possibility of letting me sleep through a few feedings so I can recover a little bit, and the wounds on my breasts can scab. Then, at each feeding, they say hesitantly that it is time, leaving the decision to me. I resent them for it, but I also scold them for giving the baby too much formula.

That night, I try pumping milk with the different pumps my husband has brought on loan from the pharmacy. The pharmacist has sold him many things with the assurance that they will relieve the pain of feeding: silicone shields and cups and pads and "natural" pumps for collecting leaking milk. They are heaped by the bedside, and soon I throw them all away in fury. The disinfected parts for the pumps are lined on the kitchen counter, overwhelming me. For some days now, my husband has been telling me he can show me how to fit the pieces together, which I refuse. It's as if he's proposing to teach me a new language. I ask him to choose one of the pumps and assemble it.

"No need to teach me anything," I snap. "Give me the machine ready to use." After twelve minutes of pumping, my eyes winced shut with pain, I discover that I've collected a literal thimbleful of milk, stained with blood from my scars, which we pour into the baby's mouth with a silver spoon.

"Look," my mother says, "You've tried everything you can. At this point there's nothing more you can do." There is something like humiliation in her tone, as if she has failed at her duty to make me produce milk. The next day, the stew is even thicker, so that a few spoonfuls are enough to fill us. My mother herself hardly eats anything.

"You need to eat," she tells me. As a matter of habit, it seems, because I'm never not eating. "If you don't eat, there won't be milk."

On the phone, she tells relatives that the baby is doing well.

"Ayşegül is breastfeeding," she says. "Of course, these first days are a little hard." There is no mention of formula, no mention that I've tried everything and might as well give up.

12.

Among objects to keep the Scarlet Woman at bay: onions, nigella seeds, evil-eye beads, horse reins, brooms, mirrors, garlic. The internet suggests bringing a white horse into the postpartum bedroom. Another source, however, warns that the Scarlet Woman also visits mares at night. For this reason, it is advised to spread tar on the animals' backs, so that the Scarlet Woman cannot mount them.

13.

There is something pathetic about a mother who cannot feed her baby. Just as with the sadness, I'm constantly searching to unearth a secret, a piece of a puzzle. If only I could decipher it, the baby would feed happily. Perhaps it has to do with the fact that I have never really liked my breasts, I consider, which hinders the flow of milk. Perhaps the baby can feel my internalized dislike. Again, the hunt for a culprit, to locate and undo. I dim the lights and burn candles in the bedroom, strip myself and the baby naked, because I read that this will increase oxytocin and milk production. I sing to the baby, who is writhing in hunger against my bare skin. Each time, I have to call for my husband or mother, to ask for their help in positioning the baby as the midwife did, in hopes she might feed peacefully as she did the other day.

The midwife comes again, positions the baby, holding her lashing head until she begins to feed. Afterward, she tells me to continue pumping, no matter the amount, then sits down to drink the sherbet. In her presence, everything is in order, the baby feeds contentedly, her eyes closed.

I name the midwife Mary Poppins, our miraculous nanny. But I don't want my mother to feel hurt that this stranger sets things right in our household. I make jokes about Mary Poppins to the baby when my mother is around.

"Listen," I say, "if you don't eat properly, I'll call Mary Poppins. She won't be gentle with you like Grandma. She'll hold your head tight and make you feed, no excuses!"

In the meantime, I'm continuing my investigation, trying to figure out some common fate that befell babies who weren't breastfed. My mother tells me about one of her best friends, fed cow's milk from birth, who likes to joke that her real mother was bovine. I have always thought that this friend is a bitter woman, and now I've found the root cause. I decide I will not give up on breastfeeding, not just yet.

"Somehow," my mother says, "we all grow up." She adds that it is an epidemic of our time. Never before has she had so many patients who do not have enough milk. The topic is extensively discussed among pediatricians, she tells me. Perhaps it's because of the availability of formula. Perhaps it's stress or environmental factors. Her words chill me. I feel that I am overtaken by a sly illness, my body poisoned by the thousand dangers of our ailing world.

14.

The first Sunday, my mother and husband go to the market. I stay home with the baby. The market is a five-minute walk. My husband will buy fish and cheese. My mother will get the vegetables and flowers, in my place. I instruct her to go to the farmer at the back, the Polish flower sellers at the very end.

"Don't worry about anything," my mother says, hardly listening to my instructions. "We'll take care of it."

My husband hands me the baby, who has just fallen asleep. Soon after they close the door, she wakes up. It's the first time we are alone. I try to conceal my terror from both of us, but the baby knows it in an instant. She begins to wail.

"All right," I say calmly, "let's see if you would like to eat." I don't think she would like to eat; she has just eaten. But I'm also disoriented by her chaotic pangs of hunger. I set up the feeding pillow, prop the cushions behind my back, position the baby's mouth upward toward the nipple, because I have never managed Mary Poppins's technique on my own. The baby's crying becomes frantic.

"Please don't cry," I plead, throwing aside the pillow. I rush her to the back room where my mother sleeps and close the door behind me, perhaps in an effort to hide myself, to lock away the great humiliation of not being able to soothe the baby. This is where my mother and husband find me, drenched in sweat, crying and rocking the baby in a frenzy. I can feel a throbbing between my legs, and I fear that my stitches have ripped. They take the baby from me. They apologize for leaving me alone; they thought the baby would be sleeping. I think there is some panic in their voices. One of them, I cannot recall whom, squats up and down rhythmically until the baby calms down. I go to the living room, not wanting to witness where I have failed. A few minutes later, I'm handed back the sleeping baby while my husband and mother empty the market baskets.

"A bouquet of daffodils for you," my mother announces. "And one for the baby."

Later that day, I ask, feigning nonchalance, how she manages to make the baby sleep.

"Oh, you know," my mother says, "I just rock and comfort her."

Of everything I share with friends in these weeks, this I will never reveal. It is too much to say—though I've been texting constantly and desperately, have felt the thickening of a pure and solid love for all the women who offer me understanding—that I cannot console my own baby. That I'm incapable of giving her comfort.

From time to time, I search the internet for an explanation, but I don't have the courage to type exactly what is happening. I try euphemisms and roundabout phrasings: *Hard time putting baby to sleep*.

I end up on mom blogs, women boasting or complaining that they alone can manage to soothe their baby—with their breast, their smell, their touch.

15.

In those days, I keep thinking about a book I read a few years ago, the autobiographical account of the French anthropologist Nastassja Martin who was attacked by a bear while conducting fieldwork among the Even people in Kamchatka. The bear bit off part of Martin's jaw and two of her teeth. In the months that followed, Martin underwent numerous maxillofacial surgeries, in Russia and in France, stitching her face—her identity—back together with a metal plate and screws, starting over when the plate became infected. In the throes of depression, she went back to Kamchatka to try and understand what had happened to her. She had become "medka," the Even name for a person who is marked by a bear and is transformed. From then on, she would be part human and part bear.

This is what I recall from the book: the sense of multiplicity, of things not quite feeling right. A search for answers with no direct route. I remember it was a hopeful book, despite the great fear. I want to go back to it, feeling that it describes perfectly what has happened to me: I have encountered another being, and have been torn apart. I am trying to put myself together, not sure how the pieces will fit back in.

When I finally return to the book, I find this passage that I've underlined on my first reading:

> On that day, August 25, 2015, the event is not: a bear attacks a French anthropologist somewhere in the mountains of Kamchatka. The event is: a bear and a woman meet and the frontiers between two worlds implode. Not just the physical boundaries between the human and the animal in whom the confrontation open fault lines in their bodies and their minds. This is also when mythical time meets reality; past time joins the present moment; dream meets flesh.

16.

During our three-hour night shifts, I read books, my nose buried deep in the pages to make out the script in almost total darkness. One of them is a murder mystery set in a picturesque New England town: a middle-aged woman who has assumed a new identity encounters a friend from her past. Another is about a gay man teaching for a year in Bulgaria, each section of the book unraveling a different type of intimacy. In one, I follow a love triangle in rural Italy under German occupation. I read holding the books with a single hand. I turn the pages rubbing them on my thigh, prodding with my nose. And I love these books achingly.

On his shifts, my husband listens to podcasts. One morning at breakfast, he tells us about a study investigating luck. He asks me and my mother: Do we consider ourselves lucky people?

As a child, I could will my luck into action. Once, on a ferry from Denmark to Germany, I won four consecutive games of bingo and a sizable check for the ferry gift shop. At first, the other passengers had cheered for me, then they started to eye me with suspicion. I remember the certainty that I would win, the deep concentration with which I seemed to materialize the numbers. I can still recall the visceral feeling with which I brought about my luck: a switch of my whole being, a channeling outward.

For a long time, I have not won anything. I am spectacularly bad at applications—for grants, for jobs. When my husband asks us at breakfast, it dawns on me with clarity that I've exchanged my old luck for something greater. I situate the waning around the time that I met my husband. I have always pitied people their marriages of convenience; negotiating terms, making do with conflicting ways. And I have often tried to hide the smugness of a perfect union, the feeling of being at home. It seems that I've replaced my stock of luck with this inner calm, lodged deep down.

"And how about you?" my husband asks my mother. She is silent. I feel she is going to cry. I want to stop the discussion, to distract us. I cannot say why exactly I consider my mother wronged in so many ways, and in need of my care. It is the reason I insist that she get a full night's sleep, that she enjoy herself in Paris. A few nights ago, my husband suggested with some exasperation that we ask my mother to do a night shift as well. It was out of the question, I said. My mother needed her rest.

"She's so tired at work," I told him. "She hardly has any holidays." And there is, also, the old mythology of my childhood: the way my mother was always tired. She has never gotten rid of this fatigue. All my adult life I've tried to alleviate it. Except that something has begun to unravel these days. The past is crashing into the present, breaking it apart, dismantling our mythologies.

Finally, my mother tells us that she may have been unlucky in some ways, no doubt referring to her marriage. But she has lucked out in the bigger ways. She became a pediatrician, she says, which was her childhood dream, against the odds of her background. And she was very lucky with her own children.

It occurs to me that I do not know the answer my husband will give. We have never really talked about this topic. He would consider himself unfortunate, I guess, in comparison to my bingo fortune. He is the type of person who gets stuck on public transport, stranded at airports, ends up lugging huge objects along unwalkable paths. I'm surprised to learn that he considers himself extremely lucky. He lists the near miraculous coincidences that resulted in his education and financial aids. The near miracle that we met each other on a campus in rural Vermont.

"If I hadn't happened to visit the professor at his office that day," he enumerates. "If I hadn't stayed with the host family that semester . . ."

The results of the luck study, he goes on to tell us, reveal that people who consider themselves lucky are also curious in life. When assigned straightforward tasks, they will make detours for no reason other than a desire to discover.

I ask my mother whom, of the people she knows personally, she considers lucky. Without a moment's hesitation, she names a family friend—a housewife who lives a suburban life in Istanbul. She and her husband often go on trips organized through tourism agencies. They have a summerhouse and a cat. The woman takes classes for self-development. She loves shopping for orthopedic shoes and practical handbags. She treats herself to a few cigarettes per week. She and her husband must be the most normal people I know. I can hardly believe my mother's choice.

"She's always in a good mood," my mother says. "She enjoys her life."

My own lucky nemesis equally surprises my husband. An artist with a large network and many grants to her name.

"You don't even like her art," my husband says. Recently, this artist confided in me her great fear of having children, because it would get in the way of her career as well as her social life. She was only getting started, she said. I wanted, perversely, to tell her that she should go for it, that there was never a right time, just as I had been told on countless occasions.

17.

Some months ago, in the glow of pregnancy, I had written to an author with a newborn baby to ask how she was doing.

"I have no words to describe what has happened to me," she wrote back, which I found an unsatisfying answer.

Now, I frantically try to remember all the phrases I've heard about new motherhood. But it seems I have never really listened to mothers, that I have never penetrated the meaning of what they were saying.

In the last weeks of my pregnancy, while reading about the mythology of the Scarlet Woman and the invisible beings that disturb a mother after birth, I decided to document my first forty days. I found this a delicious prospect, like watching a psychological thriller. I was eager for it to begin, to test my limits and emerge victorious from the journey.

I proposed to my editor to write a lecture on

invisibility. So much of life is predicated on the invisible, I said, listing areas of investigation utterly removed from birth: dreams, electricity, gravity. What I could not imagine was the messiness and entanglement, so thick it was impossible to see anything with any clarity, to assign meaning.

"I cannot help but think," my editor wrote back, "of the invisibility of the postpartum mother."

18.

I can't tell whether I'm imagining the sparkle of sadism from some mothers, particularly those whose first years of parenting were challenging. It's as if they are pleased by the desperation in my messages. The baby won't sleep in her cot! I write them. We can never put her down! Breastfeeding is so difficult!

They want more details, more signs of desperation. They say this is just the way it was for them. When I ask at what point it gets better, some of them respond cynically, even cruelly, that it doesn't.

There are the mothers who tell me that it's a matter of shifting my perspective. With the right attitude, the sleeplessness and pain will become a sort of blessing. I'm ashamed at myself for my complaints, for my healthy baby. Many of these mothers are quick to renumerate their own hardships, with the underlying insistence that they had it harder.

There are the mothers who tell me that I'm doing a great job. You are amazing! You made it this far! You are a superhero! What, exactly, do they mean? What am I doing that is so remarkable?

Nastassja Martin writes of her battle with the bear:

I do not know everything about this encounter; I shall let the assumed desiderata of the bears' world alone; my gift shall be this uncertainty. What we need, then, is to reflect on the places, creatures, and events that lie in shadow, surrounded by empty space, where we meet the experiential crux that no standard relationship can describe, that we cannot map our way out of. This is our situation right now, the bear's and mine: we have become a focal point that everyone talks about but no one understands. This is precisely why I keep coming up against reductive and even trivializing interpretations, however lovingly meant: because we are facing a semantic void, an off-script leap that chal-

lenges and unnerves all categories. Hence the
rush on all sides to pin labels to us, to define,
confine, and shape the event. Not allowing this
uncertainty about the event to remain requires
normalizing it so that, whatever the cost, it can
be made to fit into the human project.

Sometime in the future, having lost my nebulous form,
I will tell new mothers that they are amazing. That
it was just as difficult for me, if not more. That these
days will pass quickly. The fluid state, the prolonged
moment of metamorphosis, is impossible to retain.
But for now, the experience resists narrative. Nothing
rings true. For the transition from birth to mother is a
space of true wilderness, that is, a space of entanglement
which cannot be commodified. In the brief interval of
its duration, it isn't available for consumption. It's just
like the author told me, months ago: *I have no words to
describe what has happened to me.*

19.

The sleeping baby is enchanting. In the crook of my
arm, the cheeks puff out, the nose furls, the small ear,

with its little hairs, points upward. It is not-human. I have given birth to a spatial visitor. A fox. A tiny pig. An owl in the guise of a cat. I try to bring the face into focus but its shape eludes me.

"Metamorphing creatures enact the very possibility of change," writes Jane Bennett in her study of enchantment in contemporary life. "Their presence carries with it the trace of dangerous but also exciting and exhilarating migrations. To live among or as a crossing is to have motion called to mind, and this reminding is also a somatic event." Bennett argues that interspecies crossings—cyborgs, Catwoman, Babe the pig—present possibilities for enchantment and that cultivating this sentiment in the modern world is a project in ethics, a way "of rendering oneself more open to the surprise of other selves and bodies and more willing and able to enter into productive assemblages with them."

In the mornings, when the baby enters her deepest sleep, my mother comes to the living room and sits down next to me. For a few minutes, we watch the baby together before I hand her to my mother and go to sleep. The face changes constantly, twitching from smile to frown, eyelids fluttering in dreams, curled hands grasping for invisible shapes.

Watching its moment-by-moment crossings is like watching the gathering and dispersing of clouds at fast motion, their continuous becoming.

"Are you chasing squirrels?" we ask the baby, in the sliver of tender time we share each morning. Side by side on the couch, my mother and I are also easing into our new, triangulated bond, hacked apart and reforged by the baby.

"Are you hiding under oak leaves?" we question. "Where did you come from? What have you brought back from your travels?"

I have never been so close to something so strange. I want to wake up the sleeping creature and discover what is inside. But in her sleeping she is sealed off in mysterious transformation. She alone knows her own marvelous constitution.

Deleuze and Guittari propose *becoming* as an act without destination:

Becoming produces nothing other than itself. We fall into a false alternative if we say that you either imitate or you are. What is real is the becoming itself, the block of becoming, not the supposedly fixed terms through which that which becomes passes. Becoming can and should be qualified as becoming-animal even in the absence of a term that would be the animal become.

20.

Years ago, Katia told me the story of the birth of her child, in her midwife's house at the edge of the woods. After hours of labor, the midwife encouraged Katia to go out for fresh air and be alone. She made her way to a copse of trees and there squatted, moaning. After some time, forest creatures arrived to her sounds and watched her, answering her calls and sways with their own.

I have not verified this anecdote which I've recounted countless times to friends about to give birth, to encourage them in their fears of what awaits. (Oh, the confidence with which I spoke of the wilderness in the past, never having set foot in it.) There is something of the fairy tale in Katia's gathering of species, its grappling of two worlds.

After almost twenty-four hours of labor beside my helpless husband, I was finally escorted to the birth room in the early morning. Less than an hour prior, the midwife on rotation had expressed disbelief when I told her I was in great pain, and perhaps about to give birth. She told me that I had dilated only a few centimeters, and probably had a long way to go.

"You'll know when it happens," she said. "Real labor is truly painful." After she left, I crawled to the bathroom with an urge to throw up. Halfway there, my water broke and my husband rushed to the corridor to call back the midwife. I was on all fours, thrashing in pain. I banged against the walls, pounded the floor with my hands. What I remember above all is the assault of materials. The metal doors, the flecked orange light, the creamy white floors: the world become tangible, blaring in its physicality. Moments of pure present time. Later, I recalled the term "transition" I'd read in a birthing book from the sixties, denoting the passage to the final stage of labor. It was, also, a transition to animal. And it was this state of near madness, of being in between, that would stay with me for the days, and weeks, which followed.

In its proximity to the other, the transition of birth is not unlike the in-between space of the shaman in oral cultures. Just as the shaman must negotiate an order between the human and non-human worlds through his unique position as an intermediary, so the mother must traverse realms of bodily and psychic transformation to clear a new space that will harbor another being.

Writing of his studies with shamans in Nepal and Indonesia, the anthropologist David Abram argues that:

Only by temporarily shedding the accepted perceptual logic of his culture can the sorcerer hope to enter into relation with other species on their own terms; only by altering the common organization of his senses will he be able to enter into rapport with the multiple nonhuman sensibilities that animate the local landscape. It is this, we might say, that defines a shaman: the ability to readily slip out of the perceptual boundaries that demarcate his or her particular culture—boundaries reinforced by social customs, taboos, and most importantly, the common speech or language—in order to make contact with, and learn from, the other powers in the land. His magic is precisely this heightened receptivity to the meaningful solicitations—songs, cries, gestures—of the larger, more-than-human field.

In her own transition, the mother is at once shaman and patient. Like the shaman, she has become porous, shape-shifting. And like the patient whom the shaman heals with his intermediation, she is susceptible to illness, to wicked presences.

"Disease, in such cultures," writes Abrams, "is often conceptualized as a kind of systemic imbalance within the sick person, or more vividly as the intrusion of a demonic or malevolent presence into his body. There are, at times, malevolent influences within the village or tribe itself that disrupt the health and emotional well-being of susceptible individuals within the community."

One day, my mother tells me that she has a small pain in her back. She is not one to exaggerate: she has gone into active labor reading a newspaper; she once endured an infected bone for several months, with the single complaint that she didn't feel very comfortable. Immediately, I know that her pain is severe. I tell her it must be from all the cooking and cleaning. Daily, we find her doubled over, scrubbing underneath couches and beds, airing carpets out the window.

"Oh, that's nothing," my mother says. What, then, does she think is the cause?

"You know," she tells me, "I have a way of tensing up at every little thing. I think I cripple myself with all that I'm worried about."

21.

A week or two after Katia had given birth, my husband and I visited her for two days. We had no intention of having children, back then; we'd never before been in the home of a newborn. We arrived with an impractical gift for the baby, a bottle of wine, and ingredients for an elaborate meal we were planning to cook.

Katia was sitting cross-legged in the kitchen, wearing glasses that were unfamiliar to me, holding the baby. I don't quite recall the baby, too nebulous yet to discern. But I remember the feeling that a cloud had descended in the apartment and that we were all wrapped in its fog, which inhibited our sight and our thoughts.

My time with Katia had always been an occasion to talk: to tell stories and unpack their mysteries. We both loved anecdotes of the uncanny, instances of telepathy and coincidence. But this visit passed in almost total silence, all of us there in body, sitting at the kitchen table. I remember that all the dishes we prepared had to be baked in the oven—perhaps it was our instinct for comfort—and that the trays stood in line at the counter, awaiting their turn.

After we left, I would write to Katia for updates, asking whether the cloud had lifted. Much later, I read that jinn, too, are said to take the form of clouds. Amira El-Zein recounts the following story:

Once [the fourth Caliph 'Ali] noticed a child in his council who was acting oddly, and he asked, "Who knows this child?" Someone replied, "I know him. His name is 'Aws, and there is his mother." 'Ali asked the mother, "Who is the father?" She said, "I don't know. One day I was pasturing the sheep for my parents—this was before Islam—when something in the form of a cloud mated with me. I became pregnant, and gave birth to this child."

El-Zein notes that besides giving form to jinn, clouds appear in religious texts in relation to epiphanies and are also used to describe faeries.

There are many other similarities between the jinn and faeries, in their separate autonomous realms:

their mischief and malevolence, their bodies of light and air. As a child, I was enchanted by the photographs of the Cottingley fairies that caused a sensation when they were published in a magazine in 1920. Later, it was revealed that the photographs were made by two young cousins, Elsie and Frances, with cutout drawings held up by hatpins and strings.

I have always found it a shame that fairies, in their vast commodification, have become more or less synonymous with make-believe, where once they commanded areas of invisibility, inhabiting the boundaries of the human and natural. What saddens me is not so much the stripping of superstition with the knife of reason, but how this whittling away has thinned our mental layers as it has sharpened them. It seems to me that in the sheer compartments of our minds, there is little room for the invisible, and for delighting in what eludes us.

22.

I go out for a walk alone. From the door of our apartment there are two possible directions: left toward the city's periphery and right toward the heart of the neighborhood. I turn left. It is evening time, raining a cold, horrible rain. There are chestnut sellers and evening commuters and impatient drivers. I keep taking one turn after the other toward the most disorderly parts of our neighborhood, to the post office near where the highway begins. Even as I walk, I consider it a shame that I'm wasting my one outing. At the same time, I have a sense of evading the life of the city that I love. What good to see people sitting at Bobance for an evening drink, the glass panes of Café des Artistes fogged up with chatter, the new books stacked at Livre Écarlate?

I am struck by people's faces, their smudged ugliness. Everyone seems deformed, as if I'm walking under the spell of a strong hallucinogenic. But in their deformation, I can see each face as a baby: the long-ago foxes and owls and tiny pigs, sealed off in their deep time, their dream worlds, while they have simultaneously aged and deformed.

"An alteration of the relationship to the world— this is how academics define madness," writes Nastassja Martin. "How is it manifested? By a period of time, a moment, short or long, during which the borders between ourselves and the outside world dissolve, little by little, as if we were gradually disintegrating and sinking into the depths of oneiric time where nothing is settled, where the boundaries between living beings are still in flux and everything is still possible."

I recognize, also, the faces of my baby in the faces of pigeons, of dogs. Past the post office, I begin to cry, watching an old, bearded man bracing against the cold.

23.

In Turkish, we speak of "extracting" the forty days, like a sort of exorcism. My grandmothers assure me that it will all get better after forty days are *out*. One grandmother means that the baby will get better in forty days: she will cry less, she will feed calmly. Whereas the other is referring to me.

In Judaism, Christianity, and Islam, forty days mark periods of trial and transformation. Moses spends forty days on Mount Sinai to receive the ten commandments, Jesus fasts for forty days in the desert before his temptation, the Masih ad-Dajjal—an evil spirit disguised as the Messiah—reigns for forty days at the end of time.

Often, the period of trial is spent in the wilderness, as in Elijah's escape from Beersheba, on the first night of which he sleeps under a juniper tree. In the morning he finds warm bread and water left him by an angel, and is strengthened to continue for forty days and nights to reach the mountain of God.

Wilderness, in its vast and unruly territories, is a space of contradiction. It is, on the one hand, a place to cross, to overcome. In its opposition to home, it is desolate and marks God's displeasure. But wilderness also engenders meaning; one goes to it in contemplation, to unite with God in hope of transformation. "Immediately the Spirit impelled Him to go out into the wilderness. And He was in the wilderness forty days being tempted by Satan; and He was with the wild beasts, and the angels were ministering to Him."

What is the trial of the postpartum crossing? Where will mother and child emerge once they have left the wild? Must the crossing be endured or contemplated? And who, in this vast land, is the predator; who is the prey?

Jack Halberstam proposes that "wildness has no goal, no point of liberation that beckons off in the distance, no shape that must be assumed, no outcome that must be desired. . . . It cannot mean because it has been cast as that which exceeds meaning."

Halberstam is interested in wildness as the illegibility of sexuality and queerness, the body existing outside capitalist frameworks. He proposes to free wildness from colonial discourses that pit it against civilization. "The wild does not simply name a space of nonhuman animality that must submit to human control; it also questions the hierarchies of being that have been designed to mark and patrol the boundaries between the human and everything else."

Fantasies of the wild are as temporal as they are spatial, existing in a primitive *before.* Halberstam is writing against the impulse to situate the wild within a romanticized long ago, now lost to us. Similarly, the postnatal wild serves as a unique space of chaos untethered from linear history, clashing time frames with great force. I wonder whether the amnesia related to the postpartum crossing may serve as a tool for understanding its unknowability, the ways in which it escapes classification. Even as I am piecing together this account from notes I took every few days and the aid of photographs, there is, at the heart of the narrative, an immense terrain that no documentation manages to bring to life: I have no recollection of my relationship to the baby. Though I have salvaged feelings of terror and confusion, wonder and sadness and loss, I cannot recall, or define, the symbiotic feeling that early postpartum surely ushers. I am looking back to this period from my current connection with the baby—who now has a name which sticks to her, whereas before it was make-believe; who exists in the world, molding her space and relationships—and in this glance back I can see little trace of the early days. Who was it I am holding? How did we feel one another's presence? I can only recall the heightened sense of being, of being multiple, though I cannot track down the multiplicity, nor can I give it a name and species. The wild, for me, is a better entryway into this ever-blurring place than the increasingly discussed maternal ambivalence. Halberstam also proposes that his study "locates conversations and narratives about the wild in a sprawling an/archive—where the an/archive becomes a space of the unrecoverable, the lost, and the illegible." As much as maternal ambivalence offers a state of, albeit contradictory, being, wildness proposes, in Halberstam's words, an *unbeing*.

24.

In Yoko Tawada's short story "Where Europe Begins," the narrator writes a travelogue in an attempt to fill the void of her journey from Japan to Moscow. As her ship is departing from the port, she throws a streamer into the air, a last link, like an umbilical cord, to the dock:

> It became my memory. The crowd slowly withdrew, the music faded, and the sky grew larger behind the mainland. The moment my paper snake disintegrated, my memory ceased to function. This is why I no longer remember anything of this journey. The fifty hours aboard the ship to the harbor town in Eastern Siberia, followed by the hundred and sixty hours it took to reach Europe on the Trans-Siberian Railroad, have become a blank space in my life which can be replaced only by a written account of my journey.

Which is to say that any attempt to set down the wilderness is also an act of transcribing onto blankness. A vanishing umbilical cord.

25.

We had been warned that it might happen, and that it would be normal. I'd listened to the warning as a formality, like reading the safety instruction card on an airplane, locating the exit rows. But here it is: the baby has a period. The blood is dark and thick. It trickles out like a warning. My mother explains that this is the result of a drop in estrogen, a hormone that was being passed on from my own body. Nothing to worry about, she says, wiping the baby down swiftly, then folding the cloth before throwing it away. The sight is grotesque. It fills me with shame. Is it the shame of my own first period? The shame that I am responsible for causing the baby this metamorphosis into adulthood, like a transgression? Is this my blood or the baby's? The past or the future?

Every time we open the diaper, I begin to weep. After a few days, I tell my husband I cannot bear to change her.

26.

I must have talked to men in those days. My brother in New York, my father in Istanbul. Our closest friend, Zach. I must have thought about my grandfather, who passed away while I was pregnant, and whose soul I believed would enter the baby's in some form.

But I can only recall talking to other women. About pumps, about sleep, about the pelvic floor and identity—"What does it even mean?"—about night sweats and bone broth. Frantic, tender, outraged conversations. Text messages like telegrams. Like poems.

27.

In the third week of the baby's life, our friend Eng, an archivist at UNESCO, writes to ask us whether we would like to contribute a video as part of a package of recordings to send to space. It should be no longer than a minute, and should chronicle some aspect of creativity in our days.

That day, for minutes at a time—the present moment is all-consuming—we consider what such a video might look like. What is there to show of our days? Feeding, changing, holding, reading. Eating, cleaning, sleeping. Brushing our teeth, going to the toilet. Going to the pharmacy. Sometimes we shower. Eight times a day, before feeding, I microwave a cloth bag filled with lentils and place it on my breasts, so that the milk will flow more easily. After dinner, I pump milk. We record the baby's every feeding and daily weight in a notebook. Rather than a monotony of repetition, of one thing after the next, the visceral experience is of an expanding and contracting present moment that allows for no other vantage point but its own.

Would we need to add a voice-over to convey creativity? A static sound to intensify the monotonous images? Or should we let the footage do the work, moving from one silent scene to the next? There is nothing creative in the outward form of our days, even though we are living through creativity itself: we are in the reverberations of Creation, covered in stardust.

For years before I gave birth, I was obsessed with the idea of maternal creativity. I asked artist mothers endlessly when they had started working again, how their work had changed, whether they had the same capacity for concentration. My friend Marie called it my "questionnaire." I held onto an anecdote about Rachel Cusk, who had supposedly said during a reading (a friend had heard it from a friend) that if she hadn't had children, she would have remained "a minor stylist." For years, I searched for signs of my own minor style without the ultimate act of creation. And I wanted to know what I would gain artistically from birth, how it would enrich my powers.

Freud's idea of sublimation suggests that creativity is a self-defense mechanism, turning the desires of the id into artistic or scientific creation. For Lacan, this nucleus of desire, when sublimated—the Thing—is characterized by its unknowability: a void. Imaginary representation, which looks to replace this void is thus a paradox, in its attempts to veil emptiness with its own image.

Ours is not sublimation but its very source. In these days of temporal and bodily fusion, there is no image that detaches as a representation from the Thing itself, just as there is no way to see the contours of the wilderness from where we stand inside its darkness.

Ultimately, we let the discussion fizzle, though we keep saying we should write back to Eng to tell her we won't manage to make the video. But we also think it's a shame that we are passing up on the opportunity to send some of ourselves into space while we are trying to find our way on earth, in the pitch black of time.

28.

My grandmother tells me it is so much easier for me, compared to what she went through. "Just look at your husband, helping out."

She lists the times she took care of me and my brother as babies. Time that adds up to years. Time in which I refused to sleep unless I was rocked and held.

"When your mother left for a month to study for her exams, you were just a few months old. You'd wrap your arms around me so tight I could hardly breathe. Can you imagine? And I was going through menopause!"

"God bless you," I say. I mean it when I tell her that I never realized just how difficult it was to take care of a baby.

Later, I cry in the bathroom. Perhaps I am crying at the fact that my mother left me. Or at the tenderness so often lined with bitterness. Or at the desperate feeling that my exhaustion will never be enough. That this is nothing; that I, too, exhausted those who cared for me.

Mothering, at every turn, is about being mothered. Everywhere in the wilderness I hear the cries of other mothers. I call back to them, asking for help, but sometimes they can't hear me through their own cries.

29.

I can hear my mother on the phone speaking to my brother's wife in New York, who gave birth a year ago. She asks in whispers whether my sister-in-law could talk to me. I am puzzled by the request, paranoid. Why are others summoned to help? Why will my mother not talk to me about whatever it is I need to hear?

During these days, I am often taken by a feeling that there is something I haven't noticed about myself, something very close. It's a trick of perspective: I need to focus so that I can see it clearly. See myself.

Once a day, when I am changing out of pajamas and into something resembling pajamas, I look in the

mirror and examine the reflection for signs of transformation. Again, the same sleight of perspective, as
if I'm continually slipping away: I cannot quite make
out my face. It's just like looking at the baby's sleeping face, in constant change. What I see is not so
much my old features, but a feeling. Something very
naive. Something like childishness. I have become a
child in my motherhood. Perhaps it is this simulta-
neous growth and ungrowth which causes the loss
of perspective.

My sister-in-law calls me the following day.

"How are you doing?" she asks, carefully. I can't
say why, exactly, this question always makes me cry.

"Oh, sweetie," she says. She tells me that in those
first weeks, she would go for a walk with her girl-
friends to cry. "It was a really shitty time."

Then she adds, "You know, every day I love the
baby more." I think she means this as consolation,
and as permission, for whatever I may be feeling
now.

Julia Kristeva positions maternal passion some-
where between aggression and tenderness, suggesting
that "feminine sexuality takes refuge in motherhood
to live out its perversion and madness, which can
also be a way of enabling their working through."

What strikes me is that the biface of maternal passion is not solely aimed at the baby but at the birthing mother's mother and grandmother, that the postpartum space brings to focus the symbiotics of care. Again, the topography of wilderness can help to navigate this cosmos of reciprocity: a space that allows for regeneration and renewal, if only in the simple exorcism of its imprisoned spirits.

One night, cradling the crying baby in the bedroom, I ask my mother whether she had a hard time following our births. It is such a simple question, and its answer has been alluded to so many times in stories. And yet, I have never asked it outright.

"Are you kidding?" my mother says. "When your brother was born, I thought, 'All right, my life is over.'"

With that first question, stories arise from their dormant depths. It becomes a ritual, almost a game. In tears, I will ask my mother if ever she felt desperation, and she will tell me of the time after my birth when my two grandmothers were constantly arguing rather than helping her out. My mother was so ill she had no milk.

Another night, another round of crying, and my mother tells me that six months after I was born, she was suddenly so unwell that *even* my father noticed.

"It must have been depression," she says offhand-edly. "Back then you just went on with it." My father proposed going away to a lake for the weekend.

There is little time to think over everything rising to the surface. The ghosts appear, greet us briefly, then are pushed aside as the baby wakes up, cries, demands our care. It is a relief that the ghosts do not settle and stagnate. "I call this maternal experience of temporality," says Kristeva, "which is neither the instant nor the irretrievable flow of time . . . *duration by means of new beginnings.* Being free means having the courage to begin anew: such is the philosophy of motherhood."

A similar idea of constant beginnings—neither as an instant nor irretrievable flow—is recounted by Abram in his description of Aboriginal dreaming tracks:

> The Dreamtime is not, like the Western, bib-lical notion of Genesis, a finished event; it is not, like the common scientific interpretation of the "Big Bang," an event that happened once and for all in the distant past. Rather, it is an ongoing process—the perpetual emerging

of the world from an incipient, indeterminate state into full, waking reality, from invisibility to visibility, from the secret depths of silence into articulate song and speech. . . . The dreaming lies in the same relation to the open presence of the earth around us as our own dream life lies in relation to our conscious or waking experience. It is a kind of depth, ambiguous and metaphoric."

Dreamlines, like the ghost-riddled track of early postpartum, are ancestral, comprising the songs of many others who came before. Certainly, the "perpetual emerging" of ghosts in the postpartum can be more obviously related to trauma, to the ghosts of the past disturbing the present. But the framework of modern psychology is so entrenched in our ways of thinking and making sense that it seems impossible to avoid its linear logic: the goal of eradicating past grief in order to orient oneself toward the future.

Shifting this framework toward a more translucent understanding of deep time allows for another way to navigate: of multiple meanings, of an ongoing state of renewal, neither locked in the past nor aimed toward a future.

30.

One August, more than two decades ago, my cousin and I called spirits every evening. We would write out the alphabet on a piece of paper, put our fingers on a coin, and, when the coin began to quiver, ask questions, letting our fingers glide from letter to letter. Sometimes, we invited others to join: our brothers, at once skeptical and spooked; my mother, dismissive but also reprimanding of our "meddling."

One night during a sailing trip, the letters of our makeshift board spelled out an order for us to *go downstairs*. My cousin and I insisted there was no other downstairs in the small boat besides the cabin we'd already visited. The order remained the same, so we dismantled the board.

The following morning, the captain informed us that we'd anchored at Devil's Bay, name so because of the ancient tombs buried under the sea. This was an anecdote we held on to all through that summer, brimming with discovery, victorious with the immensity of the world. What was it we had proved? Something about ourselves, about life. That there was more.

In September, when we were back in Istanbul, we went to have our coffee fortunes read at a café in *Kadıköy*. When we had finished our coffees, we closed our cups on the saucers and carried them to another room where a woman with bright red hair and piercings sat on a paisley sofa.

"Have you girls been calling spirits?" the woman asked us. It wouldn't be spirits who answered our calls, she warned, but jinn. If we spent too much time with them, they might stick around for good and lead us astray.

"Jinn suggest the multifarious sublunary plane of transience and transgression," writes El-Zein. "[They] are tricksters par excellence, ambiguous and indefinite." Because of their bodies of wind, jinn are impossible to describe. Often, they trick humans by assuming the shapes of other creatures.

Other memories from that summer: the joy of being adult. Our beauty, suddenly revealed. The threshold where we stood, looking out at life ahead, at the freedom to come.

In classical Islam, thresholds were believed to be intermediary spaces that could make a person ill, even possessed, if inhabited for too long.

31.

At breakfast, my mother recounts her dreams. She is disoriented, puzzled by their relentless assault.

We are in the small flat in Istanbul where I was born. There is no running water for hours of the day. She sleeps in the back room with her mother-in-law, who has bought dainty leather boots and asks my mother to clean them.

Another dream: She asks my father to adjust the turquoise ring she has gifted me for the baby's birth, because it is too tight on my finger. She can't do it herself; she has to be at the hospital. My father takes the ring and returns with something hideous in its place. "What have you done?" my mother shouts. He says this one is much nicer, whereas the ring was so simple.

Always in her dreams there is a task, and always there are the adversaries getting in the way.

32.

My mother is leaving in a few days. Whenever we change the baby together, I start speaking in my singsong voice: "Grandma is leaving you to take care of other babies. Will you ask her to stay longer? Will you say, 'I won't sleep in the mornings if grandma leaves?'"

Finally, my mother agrees to change her ticket to leave two days later. But two days is nothing at all. Nothing has settled, nothing is easier.

All this time, we have not even managed to take a photo of the three of us: my mother, me, and the baby.

33.

It's the baby's one-month birthday, and my mother's last day. Finally, at the witching hour, we gather for a photograph. The baby is wearing a special outfit, with a ruffle collar and vest. But she cries so furiously that only her screaming mouth is visible in the photos. My mother and I are wearing sweatpants and hoodies, our faces pale with fatigue. As we are having our rotating dinner—one person holds the baby while the other two eat—my mother says that if it comes to it, she will quit her job and come back to help us. What is *it*? What must happen to us for us to ask her such a thing?

That night during my shift, I am so tired that I come to bed with the baby and stretch next to my sleeping husband. It is as if I'm filled with the exhaustion of what awaits us. I quickly realize that I will not be able to keep my eyes open. But I have been warned never to fall asleep with the baby in my arms. I finally wake up my husband. I tell him I can't stay awake. He peeks out, disoriented, from underneath the pillow, then goes back to sleep. I nudge him. I propose placing the baby between us, our hands on her body, so she feels that we are still holding her. We have also been told, in a class we took before the birth, never to do this. More and more, the teachings of this class seem irrelevant. During the sessions, the doll baby fed instinctively and appropriately from a silicone breast, slept in increasing stretches of time, let its needs be known to the mother through the release of happy hormones.

Before sunrise, my mother comes into the bedroom wearing her coat and hat. Her taxi is almost here. The three of us are huddled together in bed. If my mother is shocked, she does not say it, knowing that we must find a way to continue without her. That we have arrived at some limit.

She tells me not to get up. She hugs me, and re-peats that if it comes to it, she will return.

34.

I have not spoken of our mutual hunger, the daily crisis of our two bodies. I eat before breakfast, I eat after breakfast. Bananas with tahini. Cups of warm milk with cinnamon. Bowls of nuts and dried figs. I eat before dinner standing at the kitchen counter. Sheep cheese on rye bread. Spoonfuls of honey. The meat hanging to bones in the broth. Nothing seems to settle down. I shed all the weight of pregnancy to the constant production of milk but it isn't enough. The baby starts feeding as if she were ripping apart a carcass. When it's done, she cries. We offer for-mula, which she drinks down in seconds. We could give her the entire box of milk powder, I feel, and it would not settle her. There is a hole in both of us, unable to fill itself.

Nor have I spoken enough of the body. Every thought, every silence, every conversation enlivened by its presence. The ascending, descending aches of sitting down and standing up. The fear that something might break off or settle into the wrong place. The tenderness between my legs in the shower, which I dare to probe with my fingers only weeks after the birth. The tightening of my breasts, the sudden dampness of a shirt. The sweat blooming down my back. The constant feeling that I may burst at the seams.

Before this time, I had only known the inner focus of paying attention to the body in pain, trying to manage it in this way. Now, constantly in pain, I feel myself simultaneously stretching outward, my body leaning toward its external limb, newly raw to the world and its senses. It is a dialogue with the baby's body. In the mornings, when I shower, I begin to leak milk as soon as I hear the baby's waking sounds. I place towels beneath me while nursing, to avoid staining the couch, because the baby's suction brings on heavy contractions.

Merleau-Ponty proposes the idea of a communal flesh, a braiding together of the perceiving and perceived bodies that enable their mutual communication. Rather than objects and subjects, "living experience emerges through the symbiotic intertwining of one's own pulsing body, the overflowing, transcendent world of things, and the living bodies of others."

Similarly, Eduardo Kohn articulates an "ecology of selves" in his ethnography of the Runa in Ecuador's upper Amazon that consists of both the human and nonhuman entities of a community, as well as the spirits which help make sense of the density of the forest. Moving beyond our symbolic and dualistic thought systems, which decouple thought from its worldly referents, Kohn proposes "a kind of thought that is more capacious, one that holds and sustains the human. This other kind of thinking is the one that forests do, the kind of thinking that thinks its way through the lives of people, like the Runa (and others), who engage intimately with the forest's living beings in ways that amplify life's distinctive logics."

Why locate the metropolitan mother and child in the same wilderness as the Amazonian Runa? What interests me, in the extreme embodiment of the postpartum, is the swarm of encounters during this time: with the baby, more animal than human, more sensory than intellect, and with the invisible presences that flock to the site of birth, of new life. I find, in this liminal existence, a site for multiplicity, for experiencing the world beyond ourselves. It is a site for enchantment and renewal. It presents a possibility for redefining how we relate to the flesh of the world, and how we allow the world to touch us back.

35.

The zits on the baby's face, like a rash, sadden me beyond belief. One afternoon, the thought invades me that someone will make fun of her.

"Who would make fun of a little baby?" my husband asks, when I tell him my fears. He doesn't understand the strange loop of time. He has not seen the grown strangers with deformities on the street, who all appear as babies to me, who will not be spared harassment and unkindness. I am crying for the baby who is already adult. And for the adult who was once my baby.

I cry whenever I sing her the lullaby, the saddest one there ever was:

Little frog, little frog, where is your tail?
I have no tail, I have no tail, all day I swim in the river.
Little frog, little frog, where are your ears?

I have no ears, I have no ears, all day I swim in the river.

36.

It's only been a few days since my mother left, though it seems that months have passed. We are alone with the baby, who cries at every hour.

"Typically," my mother informs us on the phone, "colic peaks just around now." She is back in Istanbul, back at the hospital, at the operation room where babies are born day after day, their mothers wearing red to ward off the Scarlet Woman. The babies are brought back for measurements, for vaccines. Some have colic, some only sleep if they are held. From my mother's vantage point, it is a bracket in time, and it is normal. From where we stand, it extends infinitely in every direction.

I tell her the baby has cried for approximately eight hours that day. What can we do?

"Sometimes," my mother says noncommittally, "probiotics may help. And sometimes they don't."

In the evening, we go out for a walk, the baby strapped to my husband's chest. Her cries are deafening. I take out my phone to record it, to gather evidence of our suffering. An old woman passes by grunting a sound of disapproval.

"Ooh là!" another one exclaims. My husband says he's tempted to give her the finger.

Right before we arrive home, we pass by the Café des Artistes where I spot a young mother with a group of friends, her baby asleep in the bassinet. The woman is drinking wine. She has tied her hair back with a colorful bandana—a cheerful sign of her busy days. This woman is me, I realize. She is exactly how I imagined I would be with a baby. Calm and cheerful in my dishevelment. A splash of creative color holding me together while I'm out enjoying life with my friends and baby.

That evening, I write to the woman who told me she had no words to describe what happened to her: "Any colic tips?"

"OH DEAR," she writes. "WELCOME."

I tell her that when I see people hanging out at cafés with their babies it feels like I'm on a different planet.

"I feel this deeply," she responds.

The following afternoon, I shut myself in the guest room and call Katia.

"My mother left and the baby doesn't stop crying," I tell her through tears. "I can't stop crying, either." I ask if she thinks I have postpartum depression.

"I don't know," Katia says. "I mean, I'm not a doctor."

But it's clear she doesn't find this the right way to think about what is happening.

"Everything is so raw right now," she tells me. "You are so porous." She tells me I will begin to see a change at forty days. She reminds me of the cloud.

37.

El-Zein offers several accounts across cultures of supernatural beings who mate with humans and later abandon their children: the jinn queen Rawaha Bint Sakan; the wild women of the woods in Russian myths; the grandmother of the Maori demigod Tāwhaki.

"One wonders why in all these stories across the world the supernatural wife never takes her children with her," writes El-Zein. "Her love for her children seems to be different from that of a human mother."

It is tempting to read the mythology of the jinn and their assault on the new mother as a metaphor for postpartum psychosis. Instructions to never leave the mother alone for the first forty days as a way of keeping the jinn at bay align neatly with the risk of depression in this time of great change. Certainly, the myth of the Scarlet Woman devouring the mother's insides may refer to puerperal sepsis. The superstitions to protect the mother and child are nothing more than the naive attempts of our primitive ancestors to control things which we now fix with questionnaires assessing the mother's state, with perfect sanitary conditions and antibiotics. Our lives have no need for such relics, or if they do, it is only for ornament, like the evil-eye bead we have attached to the baby's diaper basket, which I adjust daily so that it's facing outward.

Still, I am resistant to the urge to explain, to bring clarity to the wilderness. What is lost, in the direct correspondence of the primitive to modern, of myth to science, is the space of imagination, of the body so easily unraveled of mystery through diagnosis. What is lost, also, is darkness, the challenge to feel our way without perfect vision, and move haltingly toward no apparent exit sign.

38.

There is a line I keep hearing from other mothers writing to me for comfort: "We were never meant to mother alone." I am told that our modern ways of birthing and care are incompatible with our species, though practically speaking, I can see no other way of mothering in the foreseeable future. At least four women have told me about the birth rites in an Indonesian village, recorded by Margaret Mead. In one video, the new mother is left to sleep for two days while her relatives take care of the baby in another hut. The footage from this other world, so different from my own, makes me feel resentful. Not only because I am yet to recover from the exhaustion of birth, but because the narrative of a long-gone order starts new life with a story of lack. It cripples the experience of motherhood from the onset.

"Affective fascination with a world thought to be worthy of it may help ward off the existential resentment that plagues mortals," writes Bennett. "That is, the sense of victimization that recurrently descends upon the tragic (or absurd or incomplete) beings called human."

It seems to me that the disorder, pain, and loneliness of the early birth story contains within it another one. That this common experience, happening everywhere in the world, is a space of fascination and wilderness, neither extinct nor rare. Its dense topography has to be navigated through the call of spirits, the metamorphosis of its fragile bodies, and the surfacing of its ghosts; traversed through the constant and myriad connections that bridge its fledgling life forms. It delivers us to the body, and insists that we stay in it, that we remember we are animals.

39.

My mother has left us an envelope with several one-hundred euro bills. A note inside says it is to hire a nanny for a few weeks while we get some rest. All day long, we answer calls from women telling us about their experiences with babies. If they begin by negotiating the hourly pay, we strike them off the list. If their voices sound unsmiling, we strike them off. If they sound meek, we strike them off. There is no one left on the list, except for Brigitte, who is the only one to laugh during the conversation. But she's already found another family.

A few days later, she calls to tell us that her sister is looking for work. She is a very gentle person; she loves babies.

The sister arrives in a light blue coat. She beams at us from the doorway, even though we are eyeing her suspiciously, the baby sleeping in my arms.

She tells me that it's apparent I have not yet recovered from the birth. And not only physically speaking, she warns. She'll bring me some herbs to boil and drink every morning and night.

We tell her the baby cries and cries. She only sleeps if we hold her.

"Babies are very simple," the sister says. "They either need changing or feeding." She has four children and two grandchildren. We'll see, it's all very straightforward.

I don't have enough milk, I tell her, adding that I do everything to bring up my supply.

"You just have to eat," the sister says. She will bring me raw peanuts which I must consume in trayfuls. When she had her babies, she adds, her breasts were this big. She shows with her hands, a significant distance from her chest.

Suddenly, I want to disclose everything to this smiling stranger. I tell her I don't always manage to console the baby when she is crying. It is my husband who is much better at soothing her. I wait for her to say that it can't be true, that I must be imagining it. Or else to be shocked.

"Of course," she says, as if nothing could be more natural. "Every caprice for maman. When a mother holds her baby, it all comes flowing out."

It was just like this with her own children, she assures me. They would cry and cry when she took them in her arms. They are grown up now, all of them here in Paris.

"And how nice to have your sister here too," my husband adds.

"Sister?"

We are horrified. We tell her about Brigitte's message, hoping there is an explanation.

"Oh right," the woman says. "She is just like a sister. Practically a cousin!"

The baby is starting to wake up, trying to raise her head. The woman extends her arms to take her from me. I give her the baby, though it seems I must not hand over my limbs to strangers, however smiling or kind.

"Hello, mademoiselle," the woman says. "You and I will get along very well."

We can go lie down if we'd like, she tells us. She has everything she needs. She looks around her.

"What a lot of books you have." It's as if she has found the cause of our distress. This is why we are so tired, so famished, so lost. And I have to agree with her. I think too much about everything. I am always reading, always in my head. I have gotten things into a tangle.

"I'm a writer," I tell her. And I cannot stop myself from talking more, pleading. "I have edits due for my novel. I haven't slept in so long. I don't know how I'll manage to finish my work."

The woman tells us it's okay. She will bring the baby to feed when it's time.

In the guest room, where we sit huddled on the small bed, we hear her talking to the baby, telling her that all this, all these books, every one of them, will one day be hers.

40.

Amanda and Emmanuel come to visit. They are the first friends to meet the baby; they have been impatient to see how it is, because Amanda is due in one month. After crying the whole morning, the baby has mercifully fallen asleep on my husband's chest. I take her from him, and this is how we greet our friends, baby asleep in my arms, candles lit, coffee brewing.

We sit around the table eating lemon cake and bread and cheese and butter. We ask our friends about world news. We ask about the country-wide strike which brought life to a halt for weeks, and of which we lived mostly unaware, save for the piles of garbage bags growing taller by the day. I notice that my husband and I are talking a bit too fast, laughing a little hysterically. And yet, I am surprised to discover that I forget about the baby for minutes at a time while we chat, that I care about life beyond the wild. Not that I have stepped out of it, but that I can recognize the shapes and cadences of another life. Yet it also seems that even if I were to step out, I would not emerge fully, that I will carry with me the dirt and leaves and boughs stuck to my body. This is the great change—that I will always contain the wild. But it may take years, if not a lifetime, to know what this wilderness means and how to navigate its vast unknown. To have words for what has happened to me.

Our friends comment on the calm of our home. They say that the baby is an angel.

They've brought us a bag of gifts. "A survival package," they call it: rice pudding, jams, cookies, scented soap. I remember the time, right before, when my husband and I had stocked up so carefully: the freezer full of broth, the cupboards packed with nuts and grains and cans. We'd bought candles, baskets, linen bags for storage, as if neatly assembling gear for a hiking trip, full of eagerness for the adventure ahead. It was the feeling that we were setting out for an endurance sport, and we were keen to make it to the end, proving our strength.

I want to pull Amanda aside and correct the impression. I feel I must warn her, tell her it is not the way it looks. She is telling me about some troubles with her pregnancy, nothing serious but still worrisome. She is concerned about the possibility of a C-section. Then she asks how I've been.

I tell her that these past weeks have been the most challenging of my life. "This is the hardest thing I've ever done," I say.

"Even harder than labor?" Amanda wants to know.

Yes, I remember this as well. The days leading up to Creation, as if birth were the only obstacle. The desire to do it right, to follow all the steps. If not irrelevant, it now seems so small, compared to life itself.

And the past, before we set foot in the wilderness, appears so tame in my memory.

WORKS CITED

Abram, David. *The Spell of the Sensuous: Perception and Language in a More-Than-Human World.* New York: Vintage Books, 1997.

Bennett, Jane. *The Enchantment of Modern Life: Attachments, Crossings, and Ethics.* Princeton: Princeton University Press, 2001.

Deleuze, Gilles, and Félix Guattari. *A Thousand Plateaus: Capitalism and Schizophrenia.* Minneapolis: University of Minnesota Press, 1987.

El-Zein, Amira. *Islam, Arabs, and the Intelligent World of the Jinn.* Syracuse: Syracuse University Press, 2017.

Fraiberg, Selma, Edna Adelson, and Vivian Shapiro. "Ghosts in the Nursery: A Psychoanalytic Approach to the Problems of Impaired Infant-Mother Relationships," in *Parent-Infant Psychodynamics: Wild Things, Mirrors, and Ghosts*, ed. Joan Rafael-Leff (London: Routledge, 2002), 87–117.

Gaines, Janet Howe. "Lilith—Seductress, Heroine or Murderer?" *Bible Review* (October 2001).

Halberstam, Jack. *Wild Things: The Disorder of Desire*. Durham: Duke University Press, 2020.

Kilic, Yusuf, and Elvan Eser. "Lohusalık Sendromu (al ana/alkarısı/albastı)'nun Eskiçağ Yakindoğu Toplumlarının Kültürlerindeki İzleri: Lilith Gerçeği." *Akademik Tarih ve Düşünce Dergisi* (October 2018): 29–60.

Kohn, Eduardo. *How Forests Think: Toward an Anthropology beyond the Human*. Berkeley: University of California Press, 2013.

Kristeva, Julia. "Motherhood Today." Transcript of speech delivered at Colloque Gypsy V, Paris, France, October 2025.

Martin, Nastassja. *In the Eye of the Wild*. Translated by Sophie R. Lewis. New York: New York Review Books, 2021.

Şimşek, Esma. "Türk Kültüründe 'Alkarisi' İnanci ve Bu İnanca . . ." *Akra International Journal of Culture, Art, Literature, and Educational Sciences* 5, no. 12 (March 2017): 99–115. Accessed through Dergi Park.

Soin, Himali Singh. "On Translucency." *Protodispatch*. Protocinema, 2023.

Tawada, Yoko. *Where Europe Begins*. New York: New Directions, 2002.

Zlatev, Jordan. "The Intertwining of Bodily Experience and Language: The Continued Relevance of Merleau-Ponty." *Histoire Épistémologie Langage* 45, no. 1 (July 2023): 41–63.

ACKNOWLEDGMENTS

Thank you to Adam Levy and Ashley Nelson Levy for the invitation to write this lecture, and for the great pleasure of thinking and working together.

Thank you to the many women who sustained my spirit in the first forty days with their friendship and care: Chiara Bellasio, Katia Nikolova Cuperin, Catherine Daly, Marie Doezema, Lauren Markham, Amanda Sarroff, Kristina Lazarević Savaş, Olivia Sudjic.

Thank you, Meg Fernandes, for the illuminating conversation about the wild and for directing me to Halberstam.

Gratitude to Maks and to my mother.

AYŞEGÜL SAVAŞ is the author of the acclaimed novels *Walking on the Ceiling*, *White on White*, and, most recently, *The Anthropologists*. Her work has been translated into six languages and has appeared in *The New Yorker*, *The Paris Review*, *Granta*, and elsewhere. She lives in Paris.

Undelivered Lectures is a narrative nonfiction series featuring book-length essays in slim, handsome editions.

01 Mary Cappello, *Lecture*
02 Namwali Serpell, *Stranger Faces*
03 Mariana Oliver, *Migratory Birds*
04 Preti Taneja, *Aftermath*
05 Joanna Walsh, *My Life as a Godard Movie*
06 Ayşegül Savaş, *The Wilderness*

Transit Books is a nonprofit publisher of international and American literature, based in Berkeley, California. Founded in 2015, Transit Books is committed to the discovery and promotion of enduring works that carry readers across borders and communities. Visit us online to learn more about our forthcoming titles, events, and opportunities to support our mission.

TRANSITBOOKS.ORG